"poetry"

A collection of poetry from 14-41 years old

Daniel Bollag

Chasing paper publications
California
Planet Earth
2009

Artists Edition print

Copyright © 2009
ISBN 978-0-578-01440-1

Chasing paper publications
4475 Meadowlark lane
Santa Barbara California 93105

Printed in the United States of America

May 2009

FIRST EDITION ARTIST PRINT - 2009

Thank you to everyone in helping me with this book. Thank you for taking the time to read these pages. They are only opinions, feelings and reflections. They are not real except to me and now, maybe to you. It really has been a long road to this point. I started writing when I was 10 or 11 years old. I am happy to have kept every scratch of paper and every napkin I ever wrote on. About 90% of the poems survived. Most of these poems have not been revised from their original flow. Nothing has been censored. I love you for just opening the book. I dedicate this book of poetry to my wife and 3 beautiful children. I would also like to thank my father and mother .

Love

Daniel Bollag

Beware this book may contain rhymes!

god and politics

i am a Jew
Neither more nor less than you
We were slaves too
Our women raped by the Romans
Our leader crucified in our home land
There is too much blood on everyone's hands
Innocent families dragged from their homes
Someone sets fire to everything you own
People stuffed like animals into cattle cars
Generations to be left with the battle scars
Somewhere showers reign vile, deadly gas on naked beautiful
bodies
Somewhere they march silently into those showers
to get clean and redeem some dignity.
Somewhere sons and daughters
are slaughtered
Their blood soaks through their mother's hands
Somewhere that grieving mother is held down
ripped into and sodomized by the man
Somewhere her bones will be used as lamp stands
Somewhere science has full compliance
of the present regime that allows a man
to become an amputee in order to see
how long it will take him to bleed to death.
Somewhere millions of people are learning
to come to terms with taking their last breath
Their flesh used for soap
Somewhere a proud people still do not lose hope

…..

i am the presence before the storm
i am a tornado trying to contain it's form
i am the wave as it breaks to a calm
i am the split moment before the dawn

i am to this Earth, born
i am to myself, torn
i am no man's pawn
i am the essence of what i understand
i am no sacrificial lamb
i am a people you call Jew
i am like an atom split in two
i am you, man

……

Like 6,000,000
Like all the new orphans
Like the absence of coffins
They came for the Jews
Now they are coming for you
They are coming for everyone
911

…..

American addiction

Oil is blood
Blood is oil
Watch close as the snake begins to coil.
Our greatest enemy is the messiah
Pick a messiah any messiah
The Jews, the Christians and the Muslims have one
Someone is wrong

Oil is blood
Blood is oil
We gather the fruit, only to watch it spoil
We would rather take our guns and shoot then retire
We set fires

where there is calm
We need a race for compassion
not an arms race for bombs
We need to be strong
Someone is wrong

Oil is blood
Blood is oil
We live 80 years, we work and we toil
We waste our lives on money, power or trying to survive
There is no man who is the last man to get out alive
We are all in this together
We must weather the storm
We waste our energy on fighting for the corpse of the extinct
We pace our humanity so fast, no one even has time to think

……

Bosnia

What is the cost?
How many lives must be lost
before we give the gift of labeling mass murder a holocaust?
I guess the world will never learn from their mistakes
I guess the world leaders can sleep at night and be fake
I guess as a Jew I shouldn't care about babies boiled in hot oil
in front of their mothers
I guess it's irrelevant that similar others killed 6,000,000

of my brothers.
I guess starvation, genocide and ethnic cleansing
doesn't matter
I guess the only important thing is whether Yeltsin
and Clinton get fatter
I suppose if a tree falls in the forest but no one hears
it, then
it's not a sin
I suppose that if we ignore murder it doesn't matter
if humans die; men
women and children

How can we do this my friend?
How can we repeat history once again?
How can we sit somber sipping cappuccino
While holes are drilled in live mothers
While their babies are posted on the tips of the drills
While the child's blood spills onto the still live
mother
We should all be ashamed!
We remain, in our silent sadistic superior cities
while men women and children must endure these
atrocities
Need I remind you
that they will come for you too
and then what are you going to do…

…..

It's not about
speaking the same language
It is about sharing the
same anguish

…..

Our flag drenched in kerosene
flies bleeding fire and dreams
A river of flames flow freely
in the July 4th breeze.
Stars rain, exploding above our heads.
We bury the last dove fore she is presumed dead:
Her blood is red
Her wings white
and her eyes, her
eyes are
blue

.....

America,
the political policy of stopping ethnic cleansing
when it becomes inconvenient, is obscene
To most of us genocide as a real and on going thing
is still just a far off bad dream

.....

America I've seen your silent sacred wars
I live by your impotent laws
I saw,
I saw the blood of my brothers and sisters drip from
your claws

......

America
your children will not inherit you
Too much blood on your hands
Land,
of the free home of the slave
what is it you crave?

America you are over 400 years old
and you still can't behave

…..

America
it has been many lifetimes
since I've seen a pure native American around
And I believe the worst has happened
without anybody making a sound
AMERICA I RESIST WITHOUT A RAISED FIST

…..

We must first find god's clit
before we can suck on it

…..

The bible, the torah and the holy Koran
These are all Books written by man

The bible, the torah and the holy Koran
These are all Books written by man

…..

The bible, The torah The holy koran, these are just
books written by Obsessive Compulsive men

These men would hate what lies within their own
grave
If they only knew about their books and how they
made us all slaves

…..

The bible the torah the holy Koran
These are all books written by man
Paper and ink
They rape us to make us think
we are at the brink

…..

We stand on the shoulders of giants
We stand on the shoulders of an ostrich
With our heads buried in the sand
We are man

…..

bible is liable

…..

If you wish to watch me bleed, at least watch me
I too have needs

…..

Humanity hides under a rock
bent over backward trying to suck it's own cock

…..

Isn't it odd
You pray to god
Machine gun in hand
Listening to your I Pod
I don't understand

…..

Humanity
Sheep asleep in a deep state of sanity

…..

2 roads diverged in the woods
I took this one
I have a daughter and 2 sons

…..

Even a quiet revolution is indeed a revolution
What comes first the revolution or the solution
How do we induce evolution at a faster pace
How can we change
when we don't recognize the eyes on our own face?
How can mankind save the human race

…..

Politics and religion are about getting
your market share
of fear

…..

Organized religion kills with such ease
Religion is a disease

…..

How many children will be martyrs
How many souls must be slaughtered

…..

Osama dropped a bomb on a
building
Bin Laden
killed women and children
So in this America we are behind you
But for all your sins America we will remind you

…..

10 little Indians decide not to be
10 little Indians ask god to be free
Being a martyr, I find it much harder to live
sometimes

…..

We live we die
We are given wings
We are not given the chance to learn how to fly

…..

The men who brought down
the twin towers
were cowards
They had no power
only a shameful final hour
They have no legacy
With blood on their arms legs and knees
they bow before god
How incredibly odd

…..

I climb the vine
I call my spine
I peel the rind
from the fruit of my mind

…..

It is legal here
It is legal there
But not in between
Don't cross the imaginary line no matter what!

…..

We are in a state of war
How many days must pass
before we are ready to ask,
will there be more?
How can we ignore the signs
The terrorists brought the battle to our shore
They raped us of our peace of mind
They left us feeling deaf dumb and blind
I will never understand the strange ways of god or man
But like a grain of sand I am a part of this land

…..

I am fragile and I am weak
I'm scared, I'm scared for my wife
I am scared for my two children
I am scared for my life
because I am a child
It is time I looked in the mirror
Somehow collectively I have also been breeding this awful hate

that we have seen of late

…..

We still have the right to our peace of mind
We still have the pleasure we can find
in each other, in our lovers, mothers, father and
brothers
We will recover
There is no other choice
There can be no other voice

…..

I don't know if you knew
Jesus was a Jew

……

I am a man
not a sacrificial lamb
I do not understand
the ways of God or
man

…..

Entrenched in circles
I am a mercury poisoned Hercules

…..

Only a coward would not step up
against the current powers
Only a coward would not step up
in this most desperate and crucial hour

…..

I do not understand the ways of God or man,
I am puzzled by the dark ages
All the blood and torture
summarized in a couple of pages
In a history book written by the biggest crooks

…..

There was God in the Garden
I saw the crack of
her ass and my
dick began
to harden

…..

Prophets trying to make a profit
Prophecies self-created on bodies mutilated
Brother can you spare a dime
Lover may I have a little peace of mind

Prophets trying to make a profit
Prophecies self-created on bodies mutilated
Stolen souls like commodities sold
So much trouble created
by little hungry people with appetites that cannot be fed
People who have no idea in what deep waters they tread
Brother can you spare a dime
Lover may I have a little peace of mind

…..

They say this is all random
Humanity in fear of the Apocalypse stands dumb

…..

I know the world is mad at Jewish people
I know it is because so many people are suffering
Everybody is trying to get a little something for themselves
I for one as a Jew feel totally connected with you
I know that if one man is without then I do not have
I know if one man is starving then so am I
I do not want any more humans to die
not white, black, Jew or anybody else from Palestine
It is time we open up our mind

…..

Mannequin, Man a kin to what?
Refusing to ride the treadmill except for 8 hours a day
For the rest I will find a way
I believe that the messiah is here today
I believe that we can find a way
The Earth is the place of my birth
The soil is the sound of my soul
Like fruit spoiled on the ground
I have found the whole
How do I fill it
Should I take another hit
I'm sick of that shit
Maybe it's time to do my bit

…..

6,000,000
brothers killed
much too much blood spilled
Never Again
The end

……

God come Home - 1983

How long have we all strayed from home
How long I have waited while my self cries
happiness
How many times have I stated happiness
in a camouflage of insecurity
in a position of the world made around me
How can the eagle soar
How can the bold lion roar in omniscient ignorance
While I must suffer the blessing of God's given
human intellect
Could it be that we are truly made in God's image
Is then God also in search of his home
Has he as well strayed so far
from his inalienable right to his soul
Is this true in truth
Is this living in a pure sense
What a pity that we are all so lost
What a pity that we have all strayed so far from
home

…..

Don't interpret my thoughts unless you have a
dictionary to my mind

…..

I find
that to live in one's own mind
can be like being blind
I find that too much time
is spent on trying to survive
Not enough on being alive

…..

Dead flowers stem from a seed
Who will lead?
Messiah I'm waiting, anticipating, masturbating
over when you will finally come
Liar, my faith is fading no ones aiding
Just Jehovah Witness persuading
Spanish inquisition, 1492
Because he was a Jew
Zaidi where are you?

….

God divvies it out in portions
Things turn out to be seen in distortion
You are told if you want more it is a sin
There are hidden passages
everywhere we turn
The only question is can we possibly, maybe Learn?

…..

I am without cosmic reverence
I have seen many, many
flying giant pink elephants
I am a man

so it seems with range
I am not diametrically opposed
to change
I try to have a fair exchange
I even rearrange
when it's necessary
I try not to eat the poison berry
until it is very very ripe
Sometimes my body feels a little
too tight.
Sometimes my soul begins to
get light
Sometimes I take flight

…..

Only the torso of God remains
after science has severed its
arms and legs.
Now what remains is an empty shell
A brief shadow of
an answer that we all believed in when we feared
going to hell

…..

Paris

Cigarettes dog shit dessert espresso and baguettes
Cigarettes dog shit dessert espresso and baguettes
Cigarettes dog shit dessert espresso and baguettes
Every day we work our way out of indentured debt
Every day I try to learn to forget

……

There are continents that need to be levitated.
There are billions of minds that need to be elevated
How long have we waited
The gate is still shut
This hypocrisy that we call democracy is still
corrupt and fucked up

…..

There are religious implications
and celestial collisions
All in all they hurt
With mirrored shoes I looked up God's skirt
I found no breasts no pussy either, only dirt
The milk had run dry
All the people just wanted a new lie or a new way to
get high,
I did not.

…..

What are the repercussions for touching
the button?

…..

Will my big white ass protect me when
the walls come tumbling down
When Humpty Dumpty fell, did he make a sound?
Who now will wear his crown?

…..

When the years have gone by
and the numbers are not
whole or thought to have

some significance where a biblical prophecy will unfold
The bullshit will lose its grip hold
When profits stop making profit on the dance
We will all have a chance

.....

America's policy is
whatever does not effect commerce
does not affect or harm us

.....

Israel is real

.....

Today I woke up with the world balancing on my shoulders
Today I woke up to find things had gotten just a little colder
Today I found out my wings were fake and were not made to fly
Today I realized it is never too late to realize all my schooling is a lie

.....

6 billion
6 billion feelings to consider
Will humanity weather this winter
of our own disconnect?
If we are not alone
will we still be cold and wet?
Will we agree to never be free?

We alone are magic
We along are the cause of
our own tragic
consequence
This is truly the hour of humanity's discontent
If we survive this extinction level event,
maybe we can finally connect

…..

You fucking liars!
We are in the generation of the messiah
The messiah is you and I.
They say it's already over.
They say we are a part of Armageddon
That's depends on us, man
Out of the rubble scratching his stubble

…..

What is going on
1/3 of my people gone
1/3 of your biblical ancestry gone
What have we done
You say you are a friend
What have you done
to see that it never happens again

……

Unbeknownst to me
I have spent much of my time
sitting around a square tree
With all the concerns of the
world on my shoulders
Dying to hold her

I sold her last night
to the gypsies
I hope God skips me
Now the angels whip me
While Neptune slowly sips the
fucking sea
Where will I bathe now?
Where is my Tao?

…..

I cannot explain the turmoil in the sky
Nor the stars in the heavens
Nor why the angels want to cry
when they were born to sing
If Love should conquer
will I then sing?

…..

Mistaken identity
I do as an entity
Realized dreams
or just confused emotions
Like waves
in the ocean
The moment it breaks
is the only real

…..

Chest breathing
Ancestors healing
Life times
Like spirals of centuries bound
Like my hands that are raw

from my ancestors
digging in the ground

…..

There are many forests without trees
There are many but we are not in need
There is no seed
There seems to only be self motivated greed

…..

I pledge a legion to the gag and to the divided states
of America
and to the republicans for which it stands
One nation with hypocrisy and just is for all

…..

May I sit
upon your
gaudy golden glamorous throne
May I taste the bittersweet blood that drips from
your tender thorns
May I wed your wicked wife whilst she mourns
May I feed on the fetus of your first born
May I love you
America?

…..

The world is becoming a ghetto
Evil has grabbed humanity
by their vanity and will not let go

…..

Fuck you, you go to war
I will stay home with the woman and children
Fuck you, you go to war
I will mind the store
I will sweep the floor
2+2 often seem to add up to 4
Though the allure of being poor
seems to be pure assurance of being inside your…

…..

Naked with my thoughts I am left to dream
Hidden in the deepest reaches of my mind
I find there are still many reasons to scream

…..

I am an island tied into every branch
I will leave nothing to chance
Every time they slaughter the innocent
I am also in it
When one of us dies one must rise

I find nothing
Nothing but worthless king
You are a failure
You are no savior
You are like a bird unable to land
You are not a man
You are Bin Ladin
You are pure sin
Souls missing something
Children
Such a sick sick sin
Where do we begin?

We begin with remembering

…..

Justice just is
Locked out of heaven by my own accord
Though vengeance is not mine
I die by my own sword
laughter is just a sign of the times

…..

Flag gag

…..

For the love of god
For the hate of a hollow soul
For all the unrecognized pain
Beauty is no sin
The holy war is within

…..

Zionist
Pacifist kicking it
Without a raised fist

…..

Lost forever
like my many spiraling ancestors
wound up from centuries of slavery and salvation

Lost forever
like all the flowers dancing in the reign

Lost like a child
I remain
drowning in the kings crown

……

So many schools
So many rules
So many unused tools
So many stubborn mules
playing the fool

…..

Woman weeping
Satan sleeping
Cities swallow
Friends follow
wallowing in their hollow greed
Who will lead
in a time where our children bleed?

…..

Life has no plot
We live we suffer and then we rot
What is the meaning of a dot
connected to no one?
A man who's father bred no son

…..

Feed the children and they will be
Seed the wilting sin and guilt
shall set you free

…..

There is a call
for us to no longer stall
In Iraq the bodies
are stacked to the wall
We took it down brick by brick
But now our hatred seems
to be beginning to stick
We are obligated to open our eyes
every day to violence
Things no longer make any sense
It is so bad that the streets are in riot
The news remains silent

….

Who agreed to all this
When did I sign on the dotted line
Maybe it was something I missed
But even the shadows of my memory, it does not exist
Maybe it is a thick rind that lay around the deep memory banks of my mind
Maybe mankind just did not have the time

…..

Is it mandatory for people to seek glory?
Is it mandatory for people to ignore me?
Is it mandatory for the waves to crash
grinding on the surface of the sea?

…..

When we win

it is not a sin.
When we fail,
it is seen as betrayal

…..

There is a focus
that is ready to choke us
if we work too hard
toward our goals of making money
or praying to our God.
There is a focus
that will certainly lead to some hocus
pocus and grab us by the throat
and choke us.
Do not be society's scapegoat
What does Mohammad, Messiah,
or Jesus knows about current events?
Do you think Jesus knows
about Iraq and all the money spent?
Does he know of Darfur where
they did not spend one cent?

…..

So many dead in the name
of religion
So much dead in the name
of tradition
So many pillars wilting away
So many slaves begging to stay?

…..

The only mountains left to

climb are those in the deepest reaches of our own
mind

…..

I am faced with the knowledge
that I am temporary
Some of what I love is
being kept from me
The universe is Big, Blue and Beautiful
But what color is the sky
when all you see in everybody's eyes
are inconsequential and irrelevant lies?
There is only one ocean left to swim
and she is deep within

…..

99 seems a long way behind
But 2001 still rings in my mind
People dead
I wonder if I'll go under
isn't that what someone said
I remember the color red

99 seems a long way behind
But 2001 still rings in my mind
There were no bodies for coffins only orphans
This type of thing happens to often

99 seems a long way behind
But 2001 is still fresh in
my mind
I had to ask myself
How much revenge was in my heart
I will not fight back

because I will not finish what I did not start

99
seems a long way behind
But 2001 is still fresh in
my mind
though I find
that time after time
I am left with rhyme and no riddle
a square cornered at
the center and split down the middle

99
seems a long way behind
But 2001 is still fresh in
my mind
Though there has been no changing of the times

…..

In Africa where the water is
contaminated and the founding fathers,
the original man is about
to be exterminated.

…..

I could never distinguish
the difference between God
the Koran and a peanut butter and jelly sandwich

…..

There is a line around the block.
They say it is profound to get into a yoga position
and suck your own cock.

…..

Time is melting
like sand into glass
The present is melting
as the future cuddles up with our past
Some say we are armed with karma
Some say we are bombarded with the
harms of silent alarms and
apocalyptic bombs

Armed with consciousness
I am blind with a sense of restlessness
On my chest is the vest cast
of love that has passed
With every breath and death
there is less left for the rest

……

A riddle with a beginning and
an end but no middle.

…..

Armed with karma
I find myself harmonizing
with things like a flower or a tree

YUMI

Longevity and balance once not even a dream
Now swinging on a pendulum with my lover I will
work as a team
It almost feels like a dream
but I am awake
So from this moment forward
I will not fake
I will not take what I am not willing to give
Instead of waiting to die, it is time to live
Instead of just trying to survive
it is now time to take the chance
It is now time to dance

…..

So tomorrow I go home
I am tired of being in Paris on my own
I can't stick my dick in her ass by phone

…..

She is reliable
Our love is ecological and viable
We do not follow the bible
We are alright with being liable

…..

She is a dream
I am the seam
waiting to be in between her
like a fiend

…..

There are rainbows closing in on me

There is a wave so big it covers the whole sea
She is with me, even when I am alone she is gift to me

…..

I am restless
but not nest less

…..

The City

The strange man is the man standing still
While everyone rushes by and I ask why
Everyone is going somewhere or getting
back home to rush to be with someone or just to be alone
I miss the beauty of my little boy's face
I miss the love and compassion in my wife's grace

…..

I am colder, colder than any cold soldier
that wouldn't hold you
when you needed me most

…..

I owe everything to my sons and my daughter
I owe everything to my wife and the cleansing
water that washes away like rain all the rapid eye moving pain

….

I rely on things that defy
my cries of loneliness
Her breasts are my
bullet-proof vest

…..

Her invisibility cloaks me
It saves me from myself
My visibility chokes and provokes me
It saves me from my wealth
I am forty
I have a daughter and
a house by the sea

…..

Strong warrior
Fiery bull
Sexy squaw
with horns like cliffs
and beautiful pale skin like the abyss

…..

How did the end happen to be?
How did we all fall within the gravitation
pull of each other?
Out of all the others in the universe
how did we become lovers?
You said it was fate
I was happy, that I was not too late
The fight I had with myself almost
killed me
She stood around and got hit and
watched the clock for years

She endured all my tears
and her own
She allowed me to strangle myself
almost till my last breath
Then dizzy and incoherent my soul awoke
a beautiful voice spoke
Are you ok Daniel…
It was you
It was me
It was Yumi

……

Within my reach
I tasted the peach
I am like a petal holding on
to the wind as it gets strong
There is a purple hue to the sky tonight
There is a place beyond the end of the tunnel
and into the light

…..

She is my only real calling.
All my other passions are just
my way of stalling

…..

The waves move through me
The wind filters the evening light
The moon dances in circles
I thought I heard her call
She was with me
I was alone
like a grain of sand that turns to stone

The river was full again
but I could not drink again
My heart was pulled again
She was my friend even then

We are on this Earth forever
Now we can bathe in the river

…..

If our shadow grew an arm
Could we love anyways and
sit in each other's calm

…..

There is an alabaster
shell that runs faster than the speed in
which it fell

….

Time climbs faster than me
Time lines my mind with
a story
I see her
She has removed her fur
Now she is naked and she
begins to purr

……

I've waited all my life
for a love like my wife

…..

I fell upon a chest
a chest of gold
with a heart beat
A breast with a soul

…..

A tear drops
A drip
through the peaks
down her mountainous cheeks

…..

Ocean sing your somber song
Allow me to float in your tranquility
for inside you is where I belong
Ocean with magnificent motion
take me where I will be free

…..

She is exotic
Her beauty is too much like a narcotic
I wonder if I pledge my love
will she become erotic

….

I am a river
I am a dream
I never quiver
at my own scream
I love my hate
I avenge myself

for loving me in hell
I am reborn with a wish
I seem to always have an itch
She is actually not a bitch
My life was very complicated
That is why I mated
There is where I was created
I am no longer hated

…..

Habitually
and instinctively I am
inclined to sit rather
than stand
I am only man
I can accept
when I won't
I will except when I don't
I live my life
to be with another
You are the other
Then I run run run
like she was some sort
of Big Bullying Brother

…..

She sings a sweet song
She searches for a self she could call her own
She wants where only winds would wander
Life, my love, my thoughts sought to squander
It seems the flowers grow
It seems that the trees have begun to blossom
and the fruit has begun to show
It seems that even in my dreams

I could not imagine the papyrus hair
dripping with rain, or the succulent with
a crystal droplet of water in her arms
She was so calm, like nature before a storm
There was chaos in her cornea
But her beautiful alabaster ass made
me want to come

…..

Another day is passed
Another moment gone by so fast
We are young but our years are fluid
She was inside but only I knew it
You are like the flower whose
scent lingers
You are a healer with
your fingers
You are a selfless soulful singer

…..

I know that I love her
She makes me feel better about who I am
I know that I will never stop to discover her
I know that I love her
She makes me feel better about who I am
That is my definition of a connection
A woman that will make you feel like a real man

She is my wife
Yumi is my life
I love you, you me

…..

She lives in a palace
She sees with a southern comfort
She is the soul in my fort
I am the life of our love
I am the knife that heals her wounds
There are 3 clouds dancing above
It is 2 hours and 14 minutes after noon

She lives in a palace
She is not callus
She is young and vibrant
I am a gun waiting to calm the herd
I am not without her, without her is absurd
I am only as good as my word
My commitment is till I die
Will you lift my leg so I can kiss the sky?

She lives in a palace
She is not Alice, she still lives here
She still wears pretty underwear and cares
She is still the sun that shines through the demons of my mind
I am still blind
She is still kind
Like the rind that comes off easy
She is me
She is you
She is Yumi

…..

Without her spirit
I can not hear it
Without her near it
I can only fear it
I can never share it

…..

I see so much by looking in her eyes
I am a man and for once
in my life I don't lie

…..

I know I am not as ugly as my
reflection
I know in the end, it is all about
natural selection
She breathes and my legs get weak
She sees me as a man who will reach the peak

…..

She is young, she is smooth
and pale like a very light Irish ale

…..

I love her
I continue to discover her
She makes me sure
She allows me to be mature
She is my nurture
She is my nature
She is the one who made you and me too

…..

Sitting waiting for her scent
Watching the mountains
Paying the rent

…..

There is unity in you and me
There is unity in what we see
There is unity in Yumi

…..

The tide is steady
The pull of the moon is already taking her time
We have nothing on the table
only what we were not able
to carry out with us
We lived in the answer of what we discussed
We strived for lives that won't expose truths that
are rude and don't mean much

The tide is steady
The pull of the moon is already taking her time
I am without a rind, just 3 blind minds looking for a
peace sign
Our spines like a vine intertwine on their climb up
the trellis
It's like anything else is
There is a fog that settles
As god breathes and the gentle wind rides with
pedals

The tide is steady
The pull of the moon is already taking her time
I agree to settle with incredible
I agree to eat everything that is so edible
I am blessed and still afraid of losing you
I am tested but not my will
I have been so rewarded for choosing you

…..

You and I
are the line that melts when the ocean meets the sky
You are my why
You are the wings that allow me to fly
You are the star
that is the center of the kaleidoscope in your eye

…..

She leads us
We are thankful
to follow
god's shadow

…..

I deprive what is alive
when I do not strive
I've arrived
when my wife
is like a rib by my side

…..

I never lied
I always tried
I will always abide
I try to provide

…..

My soul floating like a cloud
She is like the wind
gently releasing my rain

My soul floating like a cloud
She is like the wind
gently releasing my rain

My soul floating like a cloud
She is the wind
gently releasing my pain

……

My love for you is endless
There is always more, when I am afraid of less

…..

  Wedding poem

Rising
Rising like the sun
from his mother
Arms stretching like branches
with gravity not against it
Lifetimes each single moment
with every breath
with every step

Rising
Rising like the one
who is ready to love his brother
I was searching
searching like a worthless king
like a child trying to sing

I was stuck in the action of taking
when all I longed for was to bring
Perhaps it is time to crawl out from under my stone
Perhaps it is time to be stronger
to no longer be alone
Perhaps it is time to pull my head out of the dirt
Perhaps now I will feel no more hurt
One thing is certain
with all the work ahead
and all that pain behind
I think before I sink
or turn to drink,
I will have the peace of mind
to sit quietly and think about absolutely nothing

…..

10 years ago we took a vow
it still seems like just now

…..

Years past
Fears never seeming to last
A soldier peels off his face
and reveals her mask
She is past the point where she would ask
She is strong able and up for the task.

…..

Days pass, some of us ask, I don't

…..

Sentenced to birth
I search for self worth
All the while
smiling at Mother Earth
I nurture nature but I still hate me
I bleed I need
I feed on your emotions
You are a full meal
I hunger like an ocean and that's real

…..

A man is a man is a man is a man
A man is a man when he takes a stand
A man is a man if he raises not his hand
A man is a man if he understands, his woman

…..

Sitting back
Rocking in my chair
Watching the sky melt into the ocean
Watching the clouds veil the moon
She will be here very soon…

…..

I have received an invitation to the
next moment in my own life and she
is my wife sitting next to me

……

Bar none
You are the sun
You are the moon divided into circles

I am a creature of time and space
I am a part of this ongoing race
My pace has faded
No trace of hate though I made it

SANTIAGO

Should I buy a gun
Should I yell from the highest mountain that I am
the one
Should I give up my son
Should I let her run?

…..

Fatal fragrance ferments
Forever like brutal memories that no one can see
Will we ever be free
or will we always need
to bleed
to score
I put one and one together
and come up with one
I asked God forgiveness
and I received a son

….

Little girl
Blind baby born to children

…..

For a moment I am without power
For a moment I am without cause
The night is worn
Joy is coming
Soon my baby will be born
Soon I will be humming
I am left without question
I am left with only honorable mention

…..

I am cold
Like my son
I am still a stranger
Oh when oh when
will he come?
Soon they say
Each page a day thinking
I've now lived past 27
and I think I'll be singing

…..

My son is far away
One year like one day
My son is so far away
I do not know what to say
My son is so far away
I cannot find my soul to pray

…..

My sun
My beautiful son
You are only one
that I will wait for
and watch as you grow

…..

He is my salvation
He is the light outside all addiction,
He is perfection
He is natural selection

He is my son
He has simply won
He is chosen to be my sun my moon and my stars
He is soon and he is so far
He is love
He is aching
He is crying
You are in denying
You are flying
Where is the herd
that lifts up all around
Who is the fucking idiot mortal
with his feet so firmly
planted to the ground
Where is the sound
when silence ends now?

Do i turn around?

……

The city is more residential than the suburbs of my life
My son with the rhythm of Fred Astaire
My son who felt life had been unfair
My son, I can see him as the champion for all who are also there

…..

In the cycle of sun is the Earth
In the cycle of my Son is my birth
We are without worth
When we feel are without sin, there is no more hurt

……

It was a strange time
All the children marched
to the beat of Armageddon
While the elders sat in the sun
and the wise men waited
on the morrow
and I,
I had a son
A beautiful beautiful son
Nothing can compare to the joy
of watching your baby being born
And so there is no pain like
having your child leave, torn
from your arms
when all I saw in her eyes was calm

ALEX

To experience
To hear the scent
To feel my child
To smile

…..

Now I'm mentally bound
by the color of his sound
He says my name
and I will never be the same
I found peace of mind in being a father
I would not rather
life be harder again
He is my friend

…..

I am here
Sharing the oblivion
with my new born son

…..

I am constantly questioned by myself and others
about who I am
I am not famished
even with my wife and my new life I have not vanished
I have sown and now I will reap
I am no longer alone now I can sleep
How many times have I

tried to prove that I am a man
Yet here I stand with my love in hand
Oh beautiful son
Oh simple one

…..

I was there
to share her pregnancy
I was there through all 36 hours
of labor
I did what I could
I did what I thought was good.
I brought her water with ice
I wished for a daughter
but a son was so so nice
I changed his diapers
I watched him grow
I watched myself
fill into a mellow slow

…..

He is my son
He is the one and only
He is the one who will
never have to be lonely
He is a dream
I will never forget the
way she screamed

…..

Man and Woman in love
in the glory of the blazing son
We are four but we are one

…..

In these later years
I have no fears
and the joy of
fatherhood has brought me to tears

In these later years
I realized now all prophecies are self created

In these later years
I do not see the coming of Armageddon
I only see the coming of the rising son

…..

I see my son
one + one
all is done
I try not to run
Things are beginning to be fun
I believe in the game of life
I have won

…..

My father said art was like
pissing in the sand

My child said that art was
the only thing that could save man

LYLA

My baby was born
She was not torn or scorned
She was mellow like a sweet sunflower with soft
shades of yellow
She was my love at first sight
She is my dream dreamt of every night
Like a man who stands in the desert
I would die without her
She is my daughter
I have found water

RANDOM POETRY CONTINUED

Shelly – 1987

A love for the first
A sweet smile
even through the worst
Never to be wrong, nor right.
Just a radiated beauty
of which to inspire
from which I write

…..

Billy – 1992

Homosexual tendencies
Heterosexual emergencies
Excuse me while I go jerk off

…..

1985

I am the wind
Allow me to respond to the flower
who asks which hour
I will cum
to pollinate her seed

1985

Amidst the howling wind
of this cold autumn night
A leaf
landed within my sight
A leaf
some call love
A sparkle of life
that fell from above

As the sun closed its weary eyes
On this night
Inside her soft and creamy thighs
We became one

…..

Paula

Like a grain of sand
a green girl blossoms into
lustrous pearl Woman
Motherhood emerges concentrically
a pearl
Mom

…..

1984

A silent wind
swept through my heart
on one stormy night
A wind
that shook the earth

with more strength than the lightning from the sky

The wind
fluttered through my heart
until I was now a part
and I was drifting with the wind
from storm to storm

But the wind
ceased to flutter
since I was now a part
and swept into another
and whispering through one other's heart
But where am I
Where have I gone?
Amidst the wind
and the howling night
I have become a part
But in becoming have I lost my own
Have I lost my heart?

…..

1988

A man needs the touch of a soft
hand like a flower needs rain
We are all Human; Understand?

…..

Liquid nights – 1985

Dark nights fill the air with a gleam of innocence
All that is around is a trickling crystal pond
The fall leaves dancing through the air

by the winds of the heavens
by the voices of the Gods
A footstep...
A silent brush
There she stood
Hair darker than the night
Eyes lighter than the sky
She was untouched by the civilized hand
and innocent to the sins and pleasures of the flesh
Was she Human
or was she but a dream?
Did it matter?
Are we ever sure that reality is not the fantasy that
we dream?
I wanted to speak but I was compelled
to feel as if a single spoken word
would scare and poison this dream state of the night
Like a deer in the wild, she slowly moves toward
me
in a secret ignorance of fright
Ready to disappear at the fall of an Autumn leaf
As she approached, I could see the sweat on her
body
I could smell the sweet juices from inside her drip
down her legs
I felt sensations surge through my body
Brought forth into a state of ecstacy
without even the touch of her hand upon me
Confusion... Unknown?
My God!
Awoken by the electric sunrise of the city
By the glare of Dawn
roused by the spotlight of the morn.
Around me, no pond, no beauty of the night
I have awoken to a world with only cement sand,
electric stars and cellophane nights...

…..

1983

We are a part of each other's home
yet we must be on our own
Fore if there is no me
or there is no you
there will never
be an us

…..

1986

Looking over yonder window
I see the great looking glass in the sky
How it stares at me through the heavens of the night
Through it I see it all
Yet none is clear
Has all life come to this?
Can it be that this is all there is?
What about beyond?
Is there something beyond?
Through the soft night I see a world
A realm where only Love shall rule
Is it a dream?
Will sadness always prevail?
How I simmer in these shimmering clouds
Not knowing why they invite me into the sky
Could it be will Love ever rule?
Fore man will soon, exhaust himself trying
searching for that world beyond
When it really lie's
only but inside

…..

1991

The liaison of a grape
and a raisin
is a strange one indeed.

…..

My spirit lies beneath the ocean
waiting for someone to set me in motion
My ego floats in the dead sea
salt on my back, blackness with a million stars
No one can see but me
They are near and far
My spirit can hear it
Though we may never know where we are
I am free but I still wear a mask
Don't ask

……

1986

A silent tear
falls down my lover's face
A loud cry muttered in hate and anger
She gave me her all
But in return
Must I relinquish my soul?
Must I hand over my heart?

…..

1986

I search
I look for what we had
I want
I desire the love we shared
I do not want you
I want us

…..

Red Light District - 1989

A mystique boutique
owned by a girl named Sheena
or was it Kristina

I can't really remember her name
Anyways it's all the same

She had a mixture of fixtures
including a picture
where her naked breasts hung
from the wall

She spreads her butt on a chair
always quite bare
and waits for little boys to come in
She'd say left your cradle
but you seem quite able
Please hang your hat on the wall

But when the moon left the scene
the little boys could only dream
Since Kristina would throw out her rose
take the red paint off her toes

Her boutique was
closed.

…..

A rainbow of innocence shines from her eyes
as she tells her soft and delicate lies

…..

Dawn yawns
Luminous tangerine twirls
a crisp turquoise morn
Droplets of dew dance
atop a crystal mirror lake
Emerald elms shade
A lonely nude
who waits
who yearns
to taste

…..

She penetrates space; I salivate.
Rose toes tip at a tender pace
Soothing sounds of suction slip slow
aloft soft green blades of moist Earthly mane
Stray strands of curled honey drip
gently down melting mocha hips
Perched peach unfurls full fiery lips
Tongue stretched a flame stabs vestal pearl
Celestial silver scintillates over absence of light
Billowy pillows caress crescents essence into the
night

…..

The gentle touch, the silent wind
How we Love to Love
How we sing about hate
The agony of a step without your Love
is to that moment
as if the world was of no peace;
A world missing the flight of the dove
So don't ask me to sing your song
Fore I must walk in a path that is my own.
I Love you, but I also Love me
Let me Love you;
set me free

…..

A man
walked down the street one day
A quiet word he did not say
A fairy tale in his head
Went to the Madam for his palm to be read
She told me what the stars would say
The woman of your dreams you'll meet today
So on he went in search for the stars
He had checked all the streets so he went to the bars
There she stood,
hair like gold
She'd give her love for a tale told
He brought her home straight to his bed
Woke up in the dawn of morn
with a paper that read
 Had fun had to run
If you'll look to the sill
You'll see my bill

…..

She played me poker
Faster and faster he goes
Losing his mind
Trails of the blind
He follows his nose
Oh no
The door begins to close
As the fly
caught in her web
begins to cry
and all his aspirations
begin to steam from lack of contemplation
As I cut off my nose
despite my face
in light of this ace

…..

A flower will wilt when watered with dark weary guilt
On the other hand, a warm quilt will fill quill's will

…..

There were many road signs with
even more directions than one lifetime
can find
She was very kind

…..

Clouds breathing
like lions dancing
in my pupil

….

Paula

Egg
Pearl
Woman
World
Little girl
Little girl dancing

…..

All alone stoned with no home

…..

There is no room for denial
once you have walked down the aisle

…..

Round and round we go
Where we will stop, nobody knows
I turned to the rear
She was no longer there

…..

God ?
a façade ?
odd..

…..

I live to love her, yet
I regret, she gives her love to another…

…..

1987

Lost in an illusion
A maze of mirrors
Constant confusion
filled with love
laced with pain

Face to face
unresolved resolutions
The pace picks up
Faster and faster
Yet my mind remains
 non functional
inadequate
and perhaps,
even insane

…..

The end is far too close for comfort
so quickly I crawl back toward my cave
Slave!

…..

A certain doom
A one way ticket to my mother's womb
A slave to my tears
crippled by a cause
or was it

a simple case of manifested fear?

…..

Lost in a moment
working off my debt
An indentured servant
who can't let go
of the umbilical cord

…..

I have no reason for this ode
I am not breaking any code
I choose my own road
I drop a load
every chance I get
I am not finished yet
I bet on whether my as will run out
I am constantly wondering what
is it all about?
My primitive is all that I am without
I am choking on bullshit
Because it is essential to what we are about

…..

Daddy
Daddy
Cutting my balls
Locking the stalls
Racing through time
riddles rhymes
a sudden sound
a ringing chime

for 23 hundred hours has come
Yet, I regret still minds blank with slates of none

…..

Chris Love

Why God?
Why such a price
Why A.I.D.S?
Why make Chris so sick?

He's a fag and a friend,
not a freak! nor a foe.
Simply stated
Chris is the kindest man I know:
 Goodbye
The End

…..

Simplicity

To think of the sun
To think of the cloud
such a contrast
yet they live in one
So don't think of right
Don't think of wrong
Just think of the magic of the flute
Just sing a song

…..

A tear falls from my eye
My soul wishes to no longer cry

…..

The gentle touch, the silent wind
How we love to love
How we sing about hate

…..

From all the
sacrifices Love shall give
the greatest of all is a red rose,
sacrificed so that Love shall live

…..

all
alone
born a stranger
from the womb to tomb

….

A simple stranger strolls the silent city streets
Humanity has raped the man in me
eye
shed a tear
for the
woman inside

…..

A man may stand amidst millions, you see
yet still be lost alone never to be free

…..

Anger dwells deep in my fists over lack of fate
My soul cries for happiness
as my dreams quietly
masturbate

…..

A
caged bird sings
even in my own home
I am
all alone…

…..

Amazing
how the raisin
all black and pruned
Old as the flower
from which it swooned
Yet how noble in grace
How magic in taste
To think at the age of eighty
We buried this lady
six feet under
Soon she will bloom over yonder
A grape will be
A grape will be

….

A castle
A tall one
built to the sky
A king

of the mountain
Diamonds for lies

…..

She slit
or should I say
she bit her own wrist
She gave up her dream
How obscene…

…..

Born alone with no home
From womb to tomb
I am destined to live
I am destined to love
alone

…..

The lonely man
is not the man who is alone
He is the man who dwells amidst a crowd of strangers

…..

Walking through the night
in need have light
a constant contrast
a state of unrest

…..

wealth is not measured in gold
wealth is strength of soul
Wealth is Health

…..

Love is the air from which my soul breathes

…..

Lost Among
my thoughts, I cry
for I am caught

A twisted desire
locked in a cage
souls of rage
lit onto fire

…..

Womb Wound

What is the reason
you have entered my home?
Do you seek shelter
Shelter from the ongoing storm?

(The wet man spoke)
A three legged man
when faced with a stand
will quiver and crawl to his cave

But an honest reproach
from a man who needs hope
would be me

running to my grave
deep beneath your cave

…..

Her sweet shadow dances in my pupil's eye
Only blue sight in morning's night was the sky

…..

Artists Nightmare

9-5

…..

Six faces I've known
Only three can I recall
One is mine
The other time
The third and worst
is being alone

……

One day I met the most beautiful blue eyes
They sparkled as did the sun when she began to rise
I will never forget the day I realized
The devil too has eyes of blue
Blue as ice
and of equal they might entice

…..

Rage on
Rage on young man

Fore soon Knight's mare will come
Only half round the sun
and there will be Dawn

Am I really a pawn?

…..

A silhouette of sultry smoke dances
I drift deep within, my mind enhances

…..

Gaggles of old geese(r)s gag us with lack of guilt
a flower wilts

…..

I don't mean to be loud
I'm young
I'm proud
I'm strong
I belong

…..

I sang to the gods
but they did not answer back

……

I danced in the mushroom
I enhanced the plush womb

…..

I pray to the little man in my head
Watch out because the devil hasn't been fed.

…..

Used eulogies
Anonymous apologies
Sadistic strategy
Antagonistic allergy
Idiot ideology
Infection
Resurrection
Medication
Acid
Mushrooms
Mescaline
Weed
Bleed
Need
Feed me
Please so that I may
cry for just one more day
See me so I may feel when I pray
So I may touch my façade
So shadows no longer
forget God
Stronger
Self worth
Earth my church
I belong here

…..

Moaning groaning foaming corners euphoria
hysteria
Claustrophobia close to you tender love payback

Pain indentured servant unnatural elephant

…..

I am the maniac
He proclaimed with innocent eyes
Too completely sane he remained
Like the cool autumn rain, not too much pain just enough to sting

…..

Most unnatural elephant
Indenture servants
Community
Unity

…..

History - If we repeat it
we will be defeated

…..

I have been dictated by hate to live alone
It is time to claim this Earth our home
How long have we felt that humanity does not belong?
For too long the children of this Earth have sung the caged birds song

…..

No one cares
if I lay my soul bare on a cold stone slab
No one cares who pays for the tab

…..

Cover the sky
Filter my brain
Reflect in my eye

…..

Sun shining
Hopes climbing
Reaching goals
Life as a whole

…..

Melting through the turntables of time
I might wonder
I might squander
the speech
the advice
of the old mighty mime

…..

Crossing borders of haste
Living within the order hate
Loving
Hating
Perpetually fading
Our insecurities escalating
as our hopes and dreams
are shattered, ripped at the seams

…..

Shadow reflects in pupil, of mine
Tar drenched churlish Dawn yawns
thunder, as clouds covet the sun,
Only blue sight in morning's night is your eyes

…..

   Paula

My conscious stays blasting
on a tidal wave we go rafting
down the aisle of boredom
Together we said I do
I do to you
Now you do to me

…..

Young at heart
I lay down to sleep
Old in body
I must ascend with the deep

…..

   Paula

I am a man
Though I do not understand
a single thing
I tingled when she put on her ring
I am happy to be a king
even if I do not own anything
She is my wife
She is my life
She is all that I need her to be

She is as delicate as the sea
She is all inspiring
She is vibrant
She brings me
into my own as a king
Paula like a pearl
egg
woman
world

…..

Evolution of the species
We need a revolution of the species

…..

We stunted our evolution through technology.
Are we ready to exercise some responsibility?

…..

I heard a word spoke too soon
I saw Dawn rise as I awoke to the moon

…..

Are there any mountains left to climb
Are there any truths besides those that exist in my own mind
Will there be a sign when it is time

…..

A whole is more than the sum of its parts
A life is more than the moments that pull at my heart

…..

You can't have all of me
I must keep some of me in my own hands
You are my wife my family is my life
but I am my own man

…..

Was I wrong
Was I wrong to sing a song
when no one would sing along
Was I strong
Was I strong when the moments were too long
when all the space in between, were caught with people being mean.

…..

We have lived a very short time
Though we have seen so many signs
We cling to the forest branches that spring with second chances

…..

The road less traveled is now a 5 lane highway with a McDonalds and a Taco Bell
The thought of consequence is tossed aside with messianic visions of heaven and hell

The mind convinces what causes the heart to wince
and since we are nano machines, we tend to even
dream in our 5x7 cell

…..

Trees take their time to grow
Mountains crumble into the ocean
Flowers sleep and the quiet cool winds blow
echoing every emotion.

….

She is a soldier of fortune
She is colder than the one who haunts you

…..

Branches reaching
Children teaching
Relatives and friends leaching off the energy that is
mine

…..

Centuries of salvation
Slavery
Rationalized ridiculous revelations

…..

The city is asleep
The buildings are breathing
People are scattered and the light of day is leaving

……

Paris revolving
Though clearly the world has stopped evolving
The voyeurs are stalking
The tourists keep walking up and down the Champs Elysees

…..

Reason and rational rape my soul

….

Raised by a retard
old school voodoo who's who of
pseudo intellect

……

Black and white rainbows
Lacking man's fight I remain slow

…..

Paradox
Like the tick tock
of a clock
Like the humility of a rock
Like my strong long hard cock

…..

Laying low in a hazy glow
I may not come but I also may not go

…..

Milking her toes
in a silken repose

…..

Don't judge a book by its cover
Don't give up your lover
until you find another

…..

Been called a loser
Been called a dope user
I did not choose her
I only meant to use her

…..

As a man
Not a sacrificial lamb
I take a stand
And allow the woman in me to be free
…..

Femininity is the key to my creativity

…..

Socrates sold his soul for a pocket full of quarters
What will be the price for your daughter?

…..

I cannot take it any more
It hurts me down to my core

Standing on the wrong side of a closed door
My wounds are so raw
like those of my ancestors

……

I look in her eyes
and see a world
I look in her eyes
and see a little girl dancing

…..

Time after time
I come back to the line
The border between my mind and what is
happening in real time

…..

Paula

She took away all the thirst quenching rain
She showed me a whole new meaning of the word
pain

…..

In hell
Locked down like a clown
in my own mental cell
So many eyes
So many lies
So many highs
Sing soldier sing
sacred songs of silence

Bring your mute mime of a muse
Let your soul know it is time to choose

…..

Soft sanctuary
Forbidden berry
Homeless cemetery
Silence sinks
Pussy stinks
Near the brink
Can still think
What is the link?

…..

Finite
High at night

…….

Sometimes I feel lonely
Sometimes people around me tell me they feel lonely too
I do miss you

…..

The TV I see, sees me too
Give god a crown and his palace becomes a zoo

…..

A blind man creeps behind minds asleep
A silent sheep swallows such sorrow that her yesterday began to borrow on her tomorrow

…..

I was there
I saw the whole thing
I have to go though,
I fear I hear the fat lady sing

…..

Is there a way
Is there a path
One that we will not encounter our own wrath
Is there something we can say that will bring on a new day
or shall we kneel before an empty sky and pray?

…..

She swallowed my soul
When I asked for it back
She handed me a stack of cash
and said that's a wrap .

…..

I stood with three men in the room.
What a surprise to find ourselves still in the womb

…..

So many women but no one for me
So many tombs, but no dead man can see

…..

Paula

You are mother earth
I am the mountain crumbling into the sea
Fire racing through my veins
Pearls for eggs
How insane
My new baby has 2 arms and 2 legs
I love him
I will respect his sins
as well as his ability to triumph within

…..

I fear my tears scared her away

…..

I am the thorn of a dead rose
I did not mourn I suppose

…..

Waking self
I can not see the stars
Nor can I know how long or how far
we must travel before we unravel where we are

…..

I sang a song
I sang a song of a place
where the human race
can belong
A place where man is allowed to be wrong

…..

Silence never broken
Words whispered
never spoke

…..

Mistaken identity
Another blank letter sent to me

…..

Solemn silence equates to volumes of violence
I am without
Though I may shout from the buildings
I have found only strangers that say they are my siblings

…..

Human
One race
You man
Understand
My heart is hard
If I let down my guard
Will she not leave me again?
The end
I didn't mean to offend

…..

I am a tainted fruit
rotten all the way to the root
I am the prickles on the cactus

I am the grip hold in the never ending hat trick

…..

A sign of changing times
A mime with a rhyme on his mind

…..

Drowning in the sink
I can't even think

…..

I have chosen a different road
I have chosen a road with a much heavier load
I have chosen the road of turmoil
I have chosen to till my own soil

…..

She dances
My lies; romances

……

Life like a flower blooming
this dark and lonely room

…..

warm calm storm snug bug in a rug scrubbing my dirty soul in a hug

…..

I am left with nothing to say
I am left with no one to pray to
I watch the cars and the people pass me by
I see all today as some sort of lie
I am cynical, I am minimal
I am full of shit. I am dying to take a hit
I have many wives
I have had many lives
Day by day I search for pure meditation like taking
out the garbage
or reading junk mail
I have spent my life trying
not to fail only to find a tag on my forehead clearly
stating that
I am for sale
I am on my own. Everything that
I love is just a loan. Gifts to be taken away if
I should pass even one bad day.

…..

Mushrooms magical enhancing
Mind at warp speed advancing
Rodger is a freak
I am reaching my peak
He's the dirtiest bird around town
At the very least
He's a horrible beast
and certainly the dirtiest goose
on the loose I've ever found

…..

Celebration
of a divided nation
Creation

Infection
Resurrection
Protection
Essential elements
Intentional development
An indentured servant
no longer
Stronger
Chains broke
It is all a hoax

…..

All I have is
cheap thrills
I reap what I will

…..

Siamese synchronicity
Silhouettes gently pirouette
Colors separate
As holy water evaporates
Not a moment to regret

…..

Marc Rich

Assembly line of a dummy and his mimes

…..

Sacrificial Love - 1986

She sat beside me in an angry passion

in the heat of a lover's rage
Thoughts of hate and anguish
passed through her mind
as she approached by silent body
I was gone
yet my body still felt
the drop of her tears
and the breaking of her heart

As she approached me
I could sense
the sweat on her body
and the tension filling up the air
I could hear
the fatal cry of her heart
yet not a word was spoken
Drip,
went her blood
catching her tears
before they reached the ground

She was gone
yet she had become
She was with me
The end to everything she once knew
Damned to Hell for an unforgivable sin
Together we became one
Eternally locked
until the end of time

…..

Masculine mornings
Tangerine rising
Bleeding skies
Simplicity rules

when you're high

…..

god
cycles
life times
birth
death
birth
earth

…….

Coach class (plane trip – sitting next to toilet)

Amidst a herd of cattle, paranoid, cotton mouth,
frustrated, really really horny, rejected.
Lardy large mammals flock single file to the
restroom.
After feeding fumes.

…….

Journey through my past
Journey to my dead grandfather
Journey to life's last

…..

So many moments scattered
Like shards of glass shattered

…..

Plastic flowers
Masking the hours
Cowards shower in power

…..

Death came knocking but I was not home
Death came knocking but I was not alone

…..

I am free in my ignorance
I will learn and take a chance

…..

I paint what I see in meditation but not necessarily
in that order

…..

Nothing ever ends
As soon as one generation understands another
comes along
Just as full of hatred and twice as strong

…..

I listened to all
I put my fist in the wall
She heard me call
Her love was too too small

…..

I am a pebble

lost in the sand
I am a petal blowing in the wind
I am sin
I am a man

…..

Resting like a vacuum ready to consume
I have found a way to bloom without the benefit of touch

…..

I am a Jew
Who the fuck are you?
They call me the cuckoo
Today I feel 6 million killed in WWII

…….

A blind man creeps behind minds asleep
A silent sheep swallows such sorrow that her yesterday began to borrow on her tomorrow

…..

Sacred son sing your lullaby as the children cry for more
The whore has found a new place to score

…..

Fasten your seat belt
Accept whatever's dealt

…..

I live a life of my own
My soul is not a loan

…..

Everybody is the devil's advocate
When all I do is try not to hate

…..

Storms like hesitation live past their present momentum

….

Soft spoken
Balls broken
Lofts smoking
Stalls stalking

…..

My mission was a revision of my vision and a decision that ended with a head on collision and turned out just fine

…..

Vanity
Man in me
A herd of sheep asleep
in a deep state of sanity
My mirage massaged milk from my mother
I was only 13, the Rabbi could have had mercy
He hurt me

…..

Lying alone I feel no pain
But dying alone, I feel only shame

…..

1982

Seldom have I thought of this caged bird singing in the night
Seldom have I wept for beauty trapped in a sin
How many times must the caged bird sing
till we realize she is crying for help
And how many times must I feel the reprimanded hand of a sin
before we realize it is only beauty hidden within

I might cry till the silent nights turn to the morn
I might roam through the fields of a forgotten tomorrow
But never will I silence the caged bird's song
or catch a tear for forgotten sorrow
How I cry,
as the caged bird sings

…..

I live for intimacy
Lost in closeness
I can't seem to find me
Only a reflection
I am a victim of natural selection

…..

Accidental tourist
Manic whore with out a raised fist

…..

 mushrooms

Soon the room will breathe
Soon old soul's sick with guilt will leave

…..

At a rave
deep in a cave
A slave
gave
me an eloquent candy
that helped me see

……

Used eulogy
Life times in chains
Pharmaceutical philosophy

…..

Remember thin walls
so thin,
one could hear
the drop of a tear

…..

Why do I long for the meek
to be strong?
Why do I see myself as unique?
All I want is to belong

…..

Its weird man
I cannot comprehend
the end

…..

She is free
She is where she needs to be
She is me

…..

Rodger
Old soldier
White knight
Right hand
Strong Man

…..

Where am I?
Who am I?
What am I supposed to do?
Do I have a purpose in this circus?
…..

I crumbled up a piece of paper
and threw into the wind

She claimed I raped her
What was my sin?

……

Taste the nectar from the king's scepter

…..

She teased me
So I raped her
She pleased me
So I escaped her
She is me

…..

Renting or living
I am all for giving
I have seen and I have heard a little
I will meet you in the middle

…..

Somewhere minds are melting
Somewhere guilt is wilting
Somewhere a man is mortal
Somewhere a soul falls through a portal

…..

Wise woman
with the sweet scent
of fermented years

…..

There is no room
in your womb

…..

From dust to dirt
From lust to up her skirt
On this planet we call Earth
I search for self worth

…..

Perhaps it is all a game
What is my name?

…..

We give to all who are thirsty
ice cold water
We bleed our seeds into son
and daughter

……

A child I remain
Bitter blood flows through
my veins
My love like chains
A child I remain
Remembrance of anger, loneliness and shame
Moaning
Groaning
Foaming
Corners
Euphoria

Hysteria
Claustrophobia
Loss to you
Tender love
Payback
Pain
Indentured servant
Unnatural elephant

……

Art is like a tart's heart farting

…..

Sweet autumn breeze
Red yellow and orange leaves
Crisp air in my lungs
Tranquil bitter, numbs my tongue

…..

Resting comfortably
I feel no knees when I bow
In retrospect I see my future as the golden past to
what is happening now
I followed the Tao
I found a herd of sacred cow
I witnessed a multitude of miracles
without saying wow
I am simply numb
and waiting for the next time to cum

…..

Street afflicted plague

Me addicted
Vague
Visions with intent
Hurt alone hollow empty stoned
no clone though.
So why bitch and moan
Because I feel like it
Excuse me while I take another hit…

…..

Acid trip - 1994

Language lingers
Magic slips betwixt my fingers
No sleep
Sown
Ready to reap
Guilt wilts
Alone
Like mother's milk

…..

I cannot find my way home
I am still all alone
Though my body is now grown

……

Care to see near me
Fear to bleed
Tears love need

…..

Phallic fortress guard me
as my soul longs to be free
Hear her crying
Fairies flying
Lovers lying inside
Oh where oh where can I hide?

…..

Freedom
Seeds come
Need some

…..

Feeling fairy
Healing hairy
No call
No one at all
Days you fucked
Now you're stuck

…..

Friends
Man
Woman
Creation
Elevation
Revelation
Enlightenment
Heightened senses
Aware, not scared

……

Breathing, feeding each others desires

…..

Acid – 1994

Felix heals the sick

…..

Man
naked streets walking
Lamb
sacred prey stalking
A hawk sings
of freedom
A child without love needs some

…..

If I were an eagle soaring through the sky
instead of a pot head getting high
I might still lie

…..

A girl watches to see what I write;
I wonder if the cunt's got a light

…..

 pin striped suited soldier

Lucifer's last request;
a jacket, a tie and a vest

……

Fairy with wings wild and weathered
Warlock with wandering walls made of feathers

…..

Lost in a crowd
Silence is too loud

…..

Narrow roads collide
A flower that blooms
has no need to bleed or to hide
They lied

……

Sisters hand in hand
Marble heart can't you understand
Hips swing
A blues man sings
Universes collide
Strangers crawl inside

…..

The name of the game is rape and I'm trying to escape

…..

Cause and effect
Accept then respect

…..

It seems I have not had any visions
since about when I began this 9-5
I know I need to sustain, to survive,
but I no longer feel alive

…..

Retarded artist farting stardust
Lust is a must
So you better burn out
before you rust

…..

Dare I dream
Dare I scream
when I feel pain
Dare I dance
when all seems sane
Dare I answer
when all will still remain

…..

Loneliness can't follow me everywhere I go
though I know,
loneliness won't leave me the fuck alone

…..

I try to stay hurt
But every day I am getting more alert

….

Lion crying
Sinister salvation
Powerful cowards
follow hollow wallow swallow
Drowning in the shallow

…..

I feel all alone
I have searched so far and long
yet I still can't find my way home

…..

Suffering is an addiction
Armageddon is a fiction

…..

Nobody really knows
I suppose that is just the way it goes

…..

What should I do?
Who knew
that we'd let it happen again
Who said that sobriety was my friend

…..

It is a long way back from paradise
when you the roll the dice
Is hell a burning fire
Or is it a bone chilling ice

When killing people seems nice
When killing does not make you think twice

Paradise is a violent vice
Take my advice
We are not mice
We are men
If it is just a matter of just hanging your soul out for sale
Why is there so much emphasis on whether we fail?
It takes the wind right out of my sails
There are many among us that believe
that to be alive is to be afraid
I pray for peace when I prayed
On my knees I believe it is a sin to humanity to be guided by doom and disaster
There is no chance for this flower that is humanity to bloom
when everything everyone does is for the there after

…..

Surface dweller
with your rubber bands, your tie eye tulips
May I have a sip?

…..

Tonight I shoot a movie on a stranger's grave
Tonight I proclaim I am too a slave
I gave
I have no more to give
I just want to live

…..

Faint frolicking
A paint and hollow king
Concrete walls stale scaling
Graffiti
the needy
99 street
My feet failing
Wander wicked woman wailing
alone
stoned
A collage of clones
trying to find our way home.

…..

Let us be one
Simply sand which grips our souls
in the morning sun

……

Lifting less burden than before
I am still caught trying to exit the door
with limitless thought
Like an innocent school girl caught

…..

Resting gently
I have spent plenty
Erasing all this pain
Searching for empty
I do not understand
I am just a man

…..

Retarded
Crazy
Inadequate
Non functional
Dumb
Scum
Silent treatment
Stunt development
Chase a child
Wicked wild
Read what he hides
Probes deep deep inside
Medication
Education
More medication
Repressed
Depressed
Mental cell
Waterless well
Suffer success
Caged like a beast
I cease

…..

Though I understand
I am but a man
A man left here
scared and unable to share
Born, torn from her womb
I have only fear
of my inevitable doom

…..

My teeth broke on the bread
It was made of stone
I was still alone
Soon dead
Someone spoke
Blood
in the oven

…..

Energy can not be destroyed
Your enemy can not you avoid

…..

A world as ours
there are so many cowards
But also there are many flowers
like Babylon at the time of the tower
It seems human nature has turned us sour

…..

Let it be
Let me be free
Let me see reality
I welcome fantasy
I dwell in her come
As our bodies become one

…..

My fingers grip grainy ground
I put my ear to the wall
I hear the sweet sound of the fall

……

How callous is Alice now that she
Lives up high in the tower

How callous is Alice now
That she possesses the power

…..

On LSD
I feel healthy
On LSD
I am no longer
Greedy
I am stronger
Not needy
It lets me be
It lets me be me
It lets me be free
I LOVE LSD
I come from everywhere
I am no one
I see all

…..

I spent centuries locked down like a clown
I wept memories of drowning on the
ground

…..

I have seen so many dreams fall
I have seen so many screams call

for God, but no one was there
I looked up at the sun
I saw the wall
but that was not all

…..

Obsessive Compulsive Disorder – performance

I do not understand the ways of God
How he haunts
How he taunts when all that I want
is to be free
Loneliness won't leave me be
and my O.C.D.

First Trip – Blinking Wash Hands, etc…. I.L.Y.G.

I do not understand the ways of God
How he haunts
How he taunts
when all I that want is to be free
Loneliness won't leave me be
and my O.C.D….

Second Trip – Tom cruise – Blinking Twitching

I do not understand the ways of God
How he haunts
How he taunts
when all that I want is to be free
O.C.D. won't leave me be
You see I bit the fruit only to taste the rind
I will never ever escape the many rapes
that happened within my own mind

…..

There is a truth lurking in the shadows
There is a naked figure that stands inside ourselves

…..

I think perhaps awards and competitiveness
are for shallow men to keep on their shelves

…..

There is a bottleneck in the species of man
when we all simply follow what we do not
understand
…..

I have been a free spirit since I was born
A life that has never been calm
A seed sprouted in spite of facing the oncoming
storm
Now things are ok
Now I can open my arms
Now I am in her calm

…..

Through the crowded streets of my own mind
It always seems to be the beginning, the middle and
the end of sometime

…..

Absinthe
in Paris
Absence
in Paris

…..

There are stories never told
There are worries that never grow old
There is freedom
There is an alliance in the defiance of things that
will not come.

……

I had a friend
tell me of
steel flakes ripping
through his skin
I tried to remind him
the holy war
is within

……

Could God really be the
sadist who made all this
or is she kind
and have we finally run out of time

……

When will I pay back the debt?
I am not your indentured servant
I am not a sacrificial lamb
I am your child

I am a man

…..

Have I paid my debt to society
Is there any way
for me to really be free?

…..

Obsessive Compulsive

From my storms bloody dawn
I have been a pawn
Alone
In search of a home…
She lied
when I cried
I believed Eve and ate the apple
As a rule
cruel is not kind!
I see too much.
It's a real rush sometimes
I feel so blind.
I don't understand
the ways of god
I choose to be alone
Yet I regret
loneliness won't leave me be
I hate O.C.D.
I fear I will never be free…
You see I bit the fruit
only to taste the bitter rind

I will never ever escape the many rapes
that happened within my own mind

……

Human
One race
You man
Understand

…..

Sentenced to birth
I feel no one
Witness to this earth
I feel only the burn of the run

…..

I see only the sky
Why am I?

…..

It is said that amidst a calm
will arise a leader from of the nation of Islam
He will promise the people an end to famine
His royal robe will be drenched in the blood of sin

A strange unity of the ignorant, the hungry and the barbaric
A new wave way of death across all of Europe
An invasion of deadly clouds make man far and sick
Hope crumbles as sheep put their hope in a false pope

…..

I am loved
by a God that I often don't think of

…..

I walk a strong maze
only to awake in a sort of daze
I am crazed
I am amazed
at the vulnerability of man
and of god

…..

The saddest face is of
the man who won the race
Because he is out of love
He is filled up with endorphins
from the win and he is
happy that others could not keep up the pace
All he can think about is the stupid race

….

Armed with karma
I find myself harmonizing
with things like flowers
and a tree

…..

Our leaders are token
The old are broken
Nobody has spoken
Only the chosen

will get out alive
So much we face
by trying to survive
So much I can't
even think of
So much that is a blasphemy to
god as love

…..

City

Dwell in a paradox
Rows of boxes and boxes

…..

Sanctuaries of blind prophets
sing sweet songs of sacred
silence

…..

Illuminated nude angels dance joyfully on warm
cozy clouds circling the midnight moon

…..

I dwell in a 5x7 cell
I call mine, my minds own hell

…..

An ocean of eyes swallow me
She tears sacred
through my pupils sill into my soul

I am scared naked and i feel cold

…..

Stifled by a silent rifle
A rotten stench of death
circles the vulture
coming down
His claws ripping
through my body into the ground
They call it culture
They say it is profound

…..

A rainbow of
innocence shines
from her eyes
as she tells her
soft and
delicate lies

…..

I saw at last
I am
grown but
I am owned
by my past

…..

My new coinage is
replacing seduction with
plain old age

…..

I don't understand the ways of God
I choose to be alone
but loneliness won't leave me be
Why did God choose me
to be plagued with O.C.D.
I feel and I know that will never be free
I try to love but the little man in my head
will not let me rest, until all that I feel is dead

…..

Perhaps the blood represents birth
Perhaps our love represents Earth
and that alone is our universal and our celestial
purpose.
Or is it all just a circus
to entertain the sane
Yet I remain

…..

The Russian revolution is at hand
the Dawn breaks with bullets flying
a child awakes, his mother is crying
The Founding Fathers take a stand
The Kremlin crumbles
and so does my faith in man

…..

Who will chart the course
when all we know is force
Who will chart the course
when we are left with

is a huge stabbing sense of loss?

…..

I am astounded
by the principles on which civilization is founded

…..

After winning
There is no finishing
After winning
We can find a new balanced beginning

…..

I am in a constant
state of shock twitching compulsively eating our own skin
Hoping to stay alive
Hoping to maybe thrive

…..

I am in it
I have sinned so many times
I can no longer put a spin on it

…..

A deer approaches
Should I kill her?
I could eat her
drink the blood
and make art
of the bones

or should I just
leave her alone?

……

Alone home clone

…..

A red pedal dancing on the way down
A dead man with a medal is only a clown

…..

Why do we scribble
profound thoughts on the
carcass of a tree

……

How did I lose your hand?
Was it because I didn't understand?
Perhaps I am not
much of a man
but I do,
love you

…..

I lie in her arms
Her sweet whispers calm
A bird shits on my head
An aristocrat finds out his blood is red
The messiah is alive and
looking for a good time
But here comes a mime

with no intentions of being sublime
A Siamese twin within
with a passion for sin
passed on to kin
you got to win
you got to win

…..

The planet is a ritualistic situational
comedy with an absence of plot

…..

Games people play
seem the same in my dream as in the day

…..

Paula

My love
was a young lady
who unknowingly
paved the road of my future
She ripped and tore all my sutures

…..

Acid – summer of 1994

I have done so much introspection
I feel like I have had a c-section

…..

I said
I'm about to quit
right after I take
just one more hit.

…..

25th birthday

Hazy day in May
faded in the shade

…..

Silently she weeps
Silently she sleeps
While she reaps
what she's sown

Silently she rocks
and watches the clock
go tick tock
all alone

…..

I whisper in her ear
I am so near
She does not hear
or perhaps
She just does not care

…..

Desperately my dreams dry
Drowning my nipple cries

…..

Friends, artists and countrymen
Once again
it's time to play pretend
Like the air
that we share
Like the sky
that gets us high
Like the sunsets
that wipe away all regret
Like the mountains
and the ocean
Like the gold fountains
and man's emotions

…..

There is no need to bleed
when we can seed the womb
There is no need to heed
to the man's philosophy of
greed and tomb

…..

I am sick without splendor
I wouldn't recommend her
I didn't mean to offend her
I just wanted to tend to her

…..

Lost lion
Helpless crying

So much longer
So much stronger
Living
Giving
Breathing
Leaving
No grieving
Seeds sing
Lies linger
Magical fingers
Bring her
back to me

…..

Solution poisoned with pollution
A mother answers, whose son?

……

Silence never broken
Words whispered
But never spoken

……

I realized engraving what I had been saving is just a way to bargain with my cravings
Least of which, if let loose can bring everything to the brink in an instant
So why not just go on instinct

…..

I am just passing through
I thought you knew

…..

There is no place more crowded
then the crowded streets of my own mind
It always seems to be the beginning the middle and
the end of some time

…..

Rooftops in Paris

Wind blowing
through the buildings
at night howling
The voice of Paris is unique to her cry
Wind whistles through the courtyard
blurring the night air dancing through the buildings
The men on the street screaming at God
Gypsies wince near the garbage
The fresh poop stinks of a new arbitrage

…..

What one man can do another can do
Where one man goes another can follow
Even where the roads are narrow
and the bridges are hollow
with the stink of decay
Day by day in the trenches
Trying to gather inches
at 60 miles an hour
trying to scatter together pinches

……

There is a puddle in the middle of the gothic
entrance. It looks like the shadow of
a man walking at 3.30 in the afternoon.

The homeless men in Saint Germain discussing
dinner arrangements with his Demons
(howling at the moon)

……

Comsup

The business has many rewards, in self esteem and
striking certain chords.
But it is not me, it is someone else.

…..

Paula

Wife's visiting friends
This alien force has invaded my home
I am no longer on my own
I wish I were alone

……

Paula

Clouds breathing
Like lions dancing
in my pupil
egg
pearl
world
little girl

little girl dancing

…..

Paula

What horror is
the route of sorrow
Fore a forgotten tomorrow
bares no fruit

…..

Paula

I love my baby
I love God
I love life
I love my wife

…..

She dances
my lies;
romances

…..

Paula

Stuck in the middle
Fucked by a riddle
a little woman
5 foot none
who ran away
one day with my son.

…..

Paula

Paula woman of my dreams
our love defies what seems
Paula little girl dancing
in the pupil of my screams

……

Hands raw
Sitting on the shoulder of my ancestors
For all their toil and pain
We remain unchanged
Our hands covered in the soil
Our lives like sifting sands
Can we find time to stop chasing man?

…..

My thoughts caught like clouds
filtering the evening sun

……

I lost my senses
I walked till the road ended
I said sorry to those I offended

…..

I never met her
She hid inside me
like a soul without the concept of being free

…..

I am faulty and weak, my bones ache
I cannot even distinguish
what is real and what is fake
Her eyes as clear as a crystal lake

…..

There are no walls in front of me
There are no windows when you
stand alone in the sea

….

Don't you understand?
Only woman can create
Only woman can make life
in an empty plate

…..

Is she friend or foe?
I guess I will never know

…..

She is me
Me is she
We are one

…..

My papa says get a job
but I want to be eternal like a kernel

on a cob

…..

Razor edges
Rusting ledges

……

When will we begin?
He is like a bird migrating without wind
He is like a herd riddled with gang mentality and sin
We are a people waiting for our sequel
We are a people crying for things to at least feel
equal

…..

Yellow dances her own dance
as blue, orange and red light up the skies
If you don't believe, open up your eyes
you'll see
Or perhaps, your thighs
if I'm lucky and you want to fuck me

…..

A sweet shadow swallows my soul
A deep dark whole
penetrates my cold
My window reflects

…..

1982

I guess even the good boy
does not find his way home
I guess no matter how hard
we try we remain alone
I guess when my soul
is whole, then God will warm my cold

…..

1992

I grow apple trees in my apartment
on the 23rd floor window sill
I stick a vacuum in my pupil
as I exercise my lack of will

…..

Reveal
Peel your skin
Heal the wound within

…..

I dream of her in the day
I long for one word she would say
I long for her touch
I miss her so much
Sometimes I can't breathe
Other times when I leave
my soul still grieves

…..

1991

Kristina,
why did I hurt you?
God made me
My OCD

Kristina,
you own my heart
I will never feel warmth again
and I will never have a
sweeter friend than you
you are my only
without you
I am lonely

…..

Sitting on the toilet
shitting waiting for inspiration to hit

……

1994

Living in the west
Is this a test?
I get no rest
I am the poorest best
I have nothing more to confess
I'm not a whore
I have a nest

…..

Freedom
Wings Love
I think I need some

…..

I can take no more
It hurts down to my core
Standing at a closed door my wounds are so open and sore

…..

Massaging a mirage
Castrating a collage

…..

Growing older
Owing more than just a shoulder
I remain as I began a soldier at the core
A soldier without a war

……

I am scared of the dark
I am not a shark
Just a dolphin pretending to be one

…..

To swim
like a dolphin
To live
like the reptile within

…..

Myself
My psyche
My ego
My savior
The one
who controls
my every
behavior

…..

Life is about suffering
Why bother to buffer things

…..

Silence never broken
Words whispered
but never spoken

…..

Long enough
to almost feel far away
Strong enough
to see a better day

…..

Falling down closely
Things still feel like a ghost to me
Resting
Tested like a new born king
Bred to suffer

Born to sing
Things could be a lot tougher
I could be recognized for all my lies

…..

Connect on either end to make
a circle
Patience like honesty is a
learned virtue
I will never know who it
was that really hurt us
Although she said it was me

…..

I have felt this
since I began collecting shit
I'm tired
I'm a little wired
not fired
I have peace
of mind sometimes
except for when I skip my Prozac
Then I go way back

…..

Soft dreams
Silent screams
Falling in between the seams
It is not though it seems
Lost in a hollow whole
Sanctuary swallow my soul

….

You mortal
Looking at god through your portal
touch yourself
feel God
Dance with your soul.
Drop your pants, fill her whole

…..

Lining books methodically on a shelf
I was 13
I wondered what it all could mean
I touch things twice
and 300 times
I put things all in line
I felt my existence
with persistence
I was a slave
I never gave
I took
I was a crook

…..

I sing a song of six pence
My generic generation makes no sense
Life seems like a series of events
or should I say arguments

…..

The waves flat flowing flying idly by.
I see nothing but this yellow golden disk up in the sky.

…..

Are we playing with blocks
or are we trying to build
a civilization?
Are we praying on people in Iraq
or are we trying to heal
a world bent on revelation?
There is no Armageddon
I promised that to my 2 sons

…..

I am not perfect
I do not hide my flaws
behind a behavioral kerchief
I am red
I ignore the society
that surrounds me
Even though now with
two children sometimes
the pressure compounds me
Sometimes I am amazed
when I live for another day
Sometimes I am not fazed
by my extreme courage in deciding to stay

……

I am told
I can be cold
I am told
the way I'm living
I'll never grow old

…..

I try to keep giving
I'm always on the take
What I spend in the end is
never equal to what I make

…..

Shy with tender
Always trying to mend her
Alas a life
crawled to the ground
Her feelings
She found them
Nothing left to mention
Except her love has its life
And her life now love

….

So many fields
finally a flower
So my shields
now is man's greatest hour

……

She showed
and I sure did tell
She sowed, whilst I fell

…..

I gave her a dollar
She said a ten would be much better

I made her holler
She said try again, I can get much wetter
She took my heart because I let her
She danced on my grave
I never really met her

…..

Winters wild winds whispers wonderful wisdoms
while whiny wicked woman warmed me with their
wet wombs

….

Time tells the way
Tulips torn from her mother
A pearl a warm wet willow
where eggs swell
deep in the confines
of the wailing walls
of her wonderful worrisome womb

……

In the old I see the new
When you are not cold I can really
see you. You are warm and
you are kind. You are calm
but you are blind

In the old I see the new
When you are not cold I really
can see you. I am lazy.
I am crazy. Things that are silly
to most, amaze me. Yet one
of life's greatest miracles

does not phase me. I feel like I
a maze. But where is?

…..

There is doubt
There is despair
There is silence
Life has certainly
proved itself not
to be fair
I care
I share
Where oh where
Is someone here

…..

Sanctuary
Warm and wet
Wild berry
Calm debited servant
Heaven sent
Life times ferment
Words never meant

…..

My heart is hard
If I let down my guard
will she not leave me, once again
Didn't mean to offend

…..

She said I did not understand

I saw her today
I caught her holding another man's hand
I prayed
she didn't get laid

…..

I am magic
My story is tragic
All my knowledge, just a hat trick

……

We are forgiven before the fact
We have forgotten way more than the act
The TV said there is a war
The TV said we better run to the store
The threat level is high. The president is high.

…..

We are our own boss
We are tossed from loss to loss
Sometimes we are given the time
to heal from what we feel
We find our God
We do not kneel
We hear the call
We will not yield

…..

Can we fill the void
or is the best we can do just to avoid

…..

Quiet hurricane within
almost too deep to swim

…..

I've dirtied my hands
I am a man
I can understand
do or die
I am denial
not a request
it's not about how much you invest
You know, win or lose
It is not for you to choose
I'll catch you later
I have got to pay some more dues

…..

Still not sold
Sitting back comfortably growing old

…..

I am just a man
lust of my hand
I understand

…..

How can you borrow
sorrow from children
Is that not a sin?

....

Rainbow in a puddle
under my foot
I have danced
but when will I root

.....

I must confess
there is a point when I rest
that I feel good
It somehow
is no longer important
for me to be understood

.....

I search for perpetual rest
I am always awake
Life is not a piece of cake
Though I extract the exact
amount of good to make it

.....

Chest
Breathing
the rest Grieving

......

Yesterday
I felt like I was dying
Today I am so happy
I feel like crying

.....

Marooned in my cocoon
Partying on the moon
A sweet session of mushrooms

.....

I am what I've become
At least, until I change

.....

Acid 1994

I am great I am good
There is no love or pain
in the grain of a piece of
wood

....

If I went the
usual way
I would not
be where I am today

....

Culture
Vulture

.....

Crossing an elastic bridge
Bungee jumping off the side of a gift

…..

Sentenced to birth
I have search this Earth
for purpose
for self worth
in this callous collage of a
camouflaged circus

…..

Without repetition
there is almost no meditation
A logical man would say
Why repeat a feat
once it's done
Why not go on to do
another one

…..

I am celebration
I am revelation
I am constipation
I am manipulation
I am polygamy
I am arbitration
I am host
I am most
of what I once was not
I don't know who the Sheriff is
but I shot myself

And perhaps I now have wealth
for my children
I owe them some

…..

A river of reign seized my
hand and by and by
released my pain

…..

13 homeless men
A baby in a garbage can
A politician takes a stand
A poker player bluffs one good hand
Another Man claims to be
 the man

…..

There is quiet when the wave crashes
There is quiet when a great man
turns to ashes

…..

I am without rage
though I may shout
from the buildings
I have found only strangers
who are siblings

……

Santa Barbara is burning and the fiddler is on the roof
Everything I have is about to go poof

…..

When I leave
I pray no one will grieve
I pray my child will believe
that it was the right thing
Fore my soul will fly and
universes will sing

…..

From Translator
I have been dubbed traitor
From self hater
To enabler
Then unable at all

…..

I am a tainted fruit
Tainted all the way to the root
I am the prickly
on the cactus
I am the grip
on the never
ending hat trick

…..

A sign of the changing times
A mime with a rhyme on his mind

…..

Past the point to comprehend
Never lend or borrow
on tomorrow

…..

Booby died
Last week she was alive
I didn't really know my grandmother
I loved her
She has a strong soul
I remember her will to live
I remember she would always give
before she would take
But on that cold day in December
she did not awake

Boobie died
All the children congregated and cried
I guess God did not lie
Everyone must die
I didn't really know my grandmother
I loved her
Now that she's gone,
from this Earth
Today is the dawn
of her new birth
Fore her soul still stands strong
and the sweet memories
of her life and her love will carry on

…..

The hats on the bed
Your blood is red
Unless of course it's blue
and you

……

She could not guess the rest
She could not confess during
the test
She asked for less
and poured even more
then the time before

…..

I am lost in the stratosphere
I am told I am out there
I am getting old
I am lost in an atom
whose mountain is the size of my fear

…..

A strong thing is this thing
we call capitalism
The hungry died frozen
while I wrote this poem
Indian summer
It's a bummer
Help the homeless

…..

We are pawns on a chessboard in a pawn shop

When we speak out, we are regarded as thorns on
this flower we call society
What is the notoriety to being in a phone book
What is the notoriety to living on the basis of a false
book
Numbers are closing in on me
Religion is a crook that has stolen my time and my
mind for my first 20 years
 I fear religion gets a glare at my children
She will steal them too
I am a Jew
But like you I am human
I am a man
I buy my dignity in a pawn shop
I will no longer lie to get props
I will be like John Lennon and lie in bed till this
madness stops

…..

Cross section
Less then perfection
More tension
Less apprehension
Much too much to mention
Still working for my pension
and then some

…..

Lost in time
I have found
some peace of mind

With all the strength
of the eagle in my eyes

and the lion in my heart
I know now what it is like
to be a part
of someone else
I give myself
I have wealth

…..

Centuries of blind prophets trying to make a profit
Abstinent in reason
Who needs them?
A dutiful boy
An uncertain rape could
certainly become a treasure to the
human race

……

Nothing much works
Everything seems to hurt
They call you the man with the nervous breakdown
I was just 13

…..

Say it isn't so that we reap what
we sow
Where should I go
when I flow
I refuse to accept no
except when its yes
Yes I'm blessed
I failed the test
I still had the privilege to confess
I try not to stress

some say less is more
I say less is less
I am questionable at best

…..

Round and round
we go
his eyes dancing
in self
gratifying pain
A great man who
in the end will
begin in shame

…..

There is a puddle in the forest
There are roots under the ground
on which I stand
There is room for love to
conquer who we know as man
There is a gap in time that
will allow you and I to escape
There is an end to the hate
There is an end to the suffering
You are not something
if someone else is nothing
You are a bluffing king
shuffling through, who knew?

….

There were 9 Mayans in a tree
The first was the mother, the father
6 sons and a daughter

Time caught them in her ruins
Completely camouflaged with the stones of
this forgotten Mayan city

…..

Razzle dazzle
The life I lead
I get my lines
From a book I read
I am happy
I am gay
At least I think…….. I should
The book said I would

…..

An apple tree
springs a fruit
green like me

…..

How Can I think as I Feel – 1983

The mane of a stallion as he races through the wind
When shot in the thigh by reality he will soon be dead
Just as that I might rationalize what I feel and only use my head
My feelings will quiver and fall until dead.

As I think of that stallion racing through the wind
Why, oh why, he runs through the hills as nature in on
Or why lovers enchanted with romance

Watching the down going of the blazing sun
Our mind's eye can never know or ever see
But at least they live until they die and are not dead
while alive.

So listen, my friend, to what I have said
And take my advice before what you feel is dead.
When you come to that border between your heart
and your head
Let what you feel follow your heart
And let your thoughts follow your head
For in the world of rationalization
Your feelings are already dead.

…..

The Lonely Priest – 1983

Cellophane nights, looking glass dreams
Your heart beat racing through my blood
Your juices surging through my body
Your dream is my reality,
yet my vision must remain mere fantasy:

Pull me from these trenches I call
the principle from which I stand;
Fore reality can be too much for a saint
when a sinner lies so close, within my heart.
I ask to thee;
Be mine my lover
Take my head and replenish my heart.
Bring me to a place where the pleasures of the flesh
are the prayers of the saint.
And the silent suppression of one's feelings is a sin.
One night
all that I want

One night of living
So that I may be awakened form this giving hell
that I have called life.
Fore I am sure my life till now
has only been the hell for another man's deeds.

…..

I feel like crying,
I turn to my soul
she is dying
My eyes bleed tears
before god
I am naked with all my fears,
I feel so odd…

…..

An
Eagle
will peck among
the chickens for only
so long,
Ere he sings
the caged birds song

…..

Less I live beneath a tree
a green delicious apple I will not see

……

Blind man's justice

I enter her womb
A blind man not knowing what is to come.
Every step I take is a journey,
a path with a new wrath,
a walk through the land of the unknown.

Please don't judge a blind man
by the laws of men that can see.
But judge by actions contrary to surroundings.

For the truly guilty are ignorant in the ways of innocence.

.....

Dreams; the bowels of insanity coming from our mind
Dreams; The jizz from our mental orgasm
Fore sanity is but a state of mind.

.....

Love is God
God is Love
Love is inside

.....

Blind Man's death – 1983

It is a dark gloomy dusk
A tranquil sunset, one unlike I have ever felt
In all the years of my dreary old life
A footstep

A slight damper in the grass,
A sound
A sudden loud crush unto the ground
How is it that I might be blessed with another soul
after all these lonely years
If it is a man to befriend me
strike me dead oh merciful God
for I am sure I will soon awake
and the dream
will be replaced with loneliness once again
The footsteps approached
I could hear a flute
whistling sweet whispers in my ear
Singing through my pupil's sill into my soul…

…..

Uncle's death

Feeling your pain,
though I still stand sane
I love you Mom

…..

The gentle touch, the silent wind
How we love to love
How we sing about hate

…..

She walks out the door
Her shadow, follows ever so slow

…..

Aaron

Feeling your pain
though I still stand sane
I love you Mom
now
and then
then and
now
From typhoon to calm
From tycoon to a strong arm
Your tears are mine
Memories of sweet mother still
so clear, near
and fine
from the day of my birth
from the day I was born blind

…..

I live to love her, yet
I regret she gives her love to another…

…..

remember
thin
walls
so thin
one could hear
the drop of a tear

…..

1993

Will I die? cried the Fly.
No, lied the Spider
quietly weaving his web.
Kill you will
why deny? reasoned the Rabbit.
I am hungry; killing is my nature :
Haitian immigrants take a cruise to America

…..

Head Games - 1982

Life is but a series of chess games.
How strange are these games
we call parts of us and ourselves.
How I ponder over every move,
How I am in thought of the consequences
that from it will come.
For if I am playing with a master
one mistake,
is all that is needed.
Just one mistake
and the game is over.
Just one mistake and all is done:

…..

Reward 1982

When death steals my soul
will I then behold
my pot of gold

……

A cast in a play
A line of dialogue in a movie
Today tomorrow
I stay hidden
For in the heart
of every rose
lies a thorn
which mourns
for its second rate citizenship

…..

Iniki-kauai I

branched Owls cry ooow ooow, Poi dogs
howl, Horses neigh, nay. –portent.

Violent winds eratic with imperia weave into
    Iniki
        hours,
            minutes,
                seconds of
Tar drenched clouds covet sun, thundering
Jagged blades of electricity crackle off
Crystal ivory ridges, mounting foam crests of
Omnipotent blue now brown, ascend over
watching Whales.
The sky opens up, pirouettes stretch rampant
razing homes. interlaced palm roots
stretch and grip the grainy beach.
Humanity hides under a rock.
Out
of this
collage of
devastation,
Life endures, nature rejuvenates

…..

Mom - 1989

There was an old ranch
With plenty of horses
run by a maiden
with kindness not forces

Every yet morning
as the animals stayed yawning
She went down to feed
and to lead them her way

As dawn broke the day
the chickens came hoarding
since they learnt that the prosperous boarding
was to gather around by the feed

The next was the grain
which always stay lain
down by the roses
while the horses stand IN poses
while the flowers interfere with the smell

But all the chickens stood peering
as this maiden went steering
and prepared the horses, the stall
for a stroll

And in the midst of the walk
not a single would talk
except Naomi in her seat
with motions of feet
letting Carafe know her day was now complete

…..

A King of Nowhere - 1983

A king of nowhere
A beggar dancing in the street.
A smile upon his face when he bites into another mans trash.
The peasant will live in happiness if his pockets are full and
his plate is not empty.

Oh, king of nowhere, living day by day.
taking that which makes you happy and throwing away all
that may cause sadness.

I ask for the responsibility of no one.
Make me the peasant in the trash
The happy beggar dancing through the city streets
Take my head and replenish my heart;
Let me be a king of nowhere.

….

Today caged
Tomorrow saved

…..

Moon beams
Tear my heart
The end to all starts

…..

We are found
and always lost
Our life is profound
but there is always a cost

…….

Unity community
Sometimes seems like lunacy
My only wish is to be free
I have a choice but to be me
There is no one I would blame
I just don't want to play
the game

…..

There was a Mayan mountain in my
mind. The only one, so the last one
left to climb. Stone fortress swimming in the sky
on a gorgeous
moonlit turquoise night.

…..

Yucatan midnight sky

A little light shadow her face
The clouds like transparent manta rays swallowing
the moon

….

Mayan ruins

Short doorways
Stone on stone corridors and hallways
Mayan children dancing
I would make love to her
Man could she sing.

…...

She is free
She is where she needs to be
She is me

….

My brother
We will recover
When we do, we will get rid of this cancer
We will let go of our hate and anger
And realize Love is the only answer
Now is the time to stand as man on the shoulders of giants
Now is the time to have a heart like a lion

…..

Masculinity need not be afraid of crying
We are at the crossroads of humanity
We are at the crossroads of our very sanity
Love is waiting for us on the other side
I for one will not hide
I will not be swallowed by the overwhelming tide
I will continue to live my life
I will be happy to be alive
I will try only to love

I will let my ego go with the wind
I will lay down my defenses and let people in

……

I am
very lonely
Where do we go from here
Do we follow nature for a swim in the
river of Humanities interwoven consciousness
Will the drift of knowledge instinct and expression
really take us all the Way to the creator's womb
Will we then be protected from negative forces

When we get there, will the Tao lead us home?

…..

The vast ocean is upon us
The smell of the sea is on us
Filtering my brain
Cleansing my soul
Giving me back all that society raped me of
Making me feel like love
Making me a whole

…..

While walking today, my heart
broke into a million pieces
I picked up the pieces put them in my pocket and
went home.

…..

Melting like a monument that stood for centuries.
I feel there is nothing under me,
though I still enjoy the slight breeze

….

We are healthy for now
I have found the Tao
Why ask why?
I guess I am always
waiting for the next piano to
fall from the sky

…..

The world is changing
The ocean is swallowing the sand
as man wallows in the emotions at hand
The world is so temporary
I don't know if the we will ever be ready
My hand is unsteady
My anger is so petty
My skin stays shedding
As the sun starts setting over blue and green
shadows of a Mayan dream.

…..

We were born to be free
We did not have to learn how to be

…..

Living in the shelter of me
under the roots of a tree

…..

In the many cycles of life and death
Even the greatest accomplishment is merely a breath

…..

I was only a figment
A variation lost in the vast pigment
I am a rain drop without a parachute

…..

We have not been put here to pretend
We have been put here to transcend

…..

Lonely, only I sat a moment in time thinking god's eye blinking

…...

7/3/06 3:45 PM

I am ready to go back to before
the race began

I am ready (again), for who I really am

…..

I am a simple and primitive man
I chisel at the rock, in hope that someone will understand.

www.ingramcontent.com/pod-product-compliance
Lightning Source LLC
Chambersburg PA
CBHW031642040426
42453CB00006B/185